I0781782

The REAL DEAL

Heather Deal

Dream Homes
YOUR DREAM. OUR TEAM.

www.hteamdreamhomes.com

The REAL DEAL:
Real Answers to Real Questions When Buying Your First Home

Copyright © 2024 by Heather Nicole Deal

Published by **H Team Dream Homes**
1602 S. Saint Andrews Rd. E., Winona Lake, Indiana USA 46590
www.hteamdreamhomes.com

Book design copyright © 2024 by Marc Thomas Eckel
All rights reserved
Cover design by Marc Eckel for Blue Spaghetti LLC
Heather Deal photos by Jamie Johnson of
    Signature Studio Photography, Winona Lake, IN

Published in the United States of America

Dedication

This book is dedicated to the dreamers,
who envision life within the walls of a new home
and to their lifelong memories
which are soon to begin.

Acknowledgements

Special thanks to lender Crystal Wilson
from The Mortgage Exchange.
crystal.wilson@themortgageexchange.com
themortgageexchange.com
260.341.3251

Thanks to Snowden and Susan Leftwich
from Athens, Texas.
You know why.

Table of Contents

Introduction

There are few things that we all long for:

Everyone wants to be loved.

Everyone wants to be needed.

And everyone wants to find their place in this world.

Surely you are familiar with the plea of a young girl named Dorothy. After closing her eyes and clicking her heels, she expressed one sincere thought over and over again:

"There's no place like home.
There's no place like home.
There's no place like home."

She longed for her place in this world. She could have simply stated personal truth, "There's no place like Kansas."

Upon looking in her house you might have found a sign, reading: "Home Sweet Home".

I cannot imagine a sign that reads: "Home Sour Home". No one wants to find themselves there. Home should be a place of love, joy, comfort, safety, security, family, and fond memories.

For each of us, home is where we find ourselves each day. It is where we rise each morning and rest each night. It is our place in this world.

When everything settles, it is where we land. Some think of land simply as dirt, the ground we walk upon. But our land, our property, is where we find our home, our estate. And it is a real estate indeed.

Purchasing a first home is often met with many questions. How does this work? What are the steps I need to take? Who can help me navigate through all the puzzle pieces of the process?

This book will help you look at real answers to real questions along your journey toward becoming a first-time homeowner.

Will you find the answers to every question in the home buying journey here? Surely not, as there are variables in the industry that are always subject to change. But this guide book will lead you in the right direction giving you an overview of what to expect.

In my years as a real estate agent, managing my own brokerage, I have shared the information found in this book with many who now know:

There's no place like home.

Together, let's make this a reality for you as well.

— *Heather Deal*

Chapter One: The Ride and the Race

Click. Click. Click. Click.

It's the sound of anticipation. You are belted in and ready to go. Up until now, you have only heard about the thrills this ride will bring. But now it's real. This is **the Real Deal.**

You are about to experience the ups and downs of a roller coaster ride that will be exhilarating and exciting. It might even take your breath away. The ride will conclude with smiles, joy and happiness. You will be glad you took the ride.

And now you are climbing that first incline.

Click. Click. Click. Click.

Ready to enjoy the ride? *Hold on.* **Here we go!**

The first question a good real estate agent will ask their client is this: What are **you** looking for in a home?

Every house has to have bedrooms, bathrooms, a kitchen… you know, the basics. But for many there are non-negotiable essentials that are also personally important. These desires need to be defined.

Consider if your list contains some of these characteristics:
- A basement
- A garage
- An out building
- Acreage
- A fenced-in yard for pets
- A newer house (or older house)
- A one-level ranch style home to avoid stairs
- A swimming pool

- A patio or deck
- A walk-in pantry
- Walk-in closets
- A specific neighborhood
- Location in a specific school district
- Location in close proximity
  to school or work

Surely the list could go on and on. Everyone has very specific ideas in mind that they are looking for. But before we get too carried away, let's discuss what is of utmost importance: **your budget**.

What we want and what we can afford may be two different things. So let's tackle the issues of budget so we can start thinking realistically about what makes practical sense.

Keep in mind what is associated with your budget and the purchase of a home:

- Your monthly mortgage payment
- Property taxes
- Homeowner's insurance
- Utilities (gas and electric)
- Water
- Trash Service
- Potential Homeowner's Association fees

And, of course, other financial obligations like your car, insurance, food, clothing, school expenses, and entertainment all need to be considered to define your complete financial budgetary needs.

With this in mind, will you be able to afford everything you want? Only you can tell. But being realistic is important. Some of your wants may need to be narrowed down and prioritized. Be prepared for a little give and take.

Now, based on the truth of all of this, we can start searching with, perhaps, more defined requirements within the parameters of what you can afford.

Please understand, this adventure is not only a roller coaster ride, it is also a race. You have already stepped into the starting blocks by dreaming of your new home. You have heard the starter's pistol and have sprung into action by beginning the process – ***the race is on!***

But as you gain momentum, you look up to realize this race is not the 100-meter dash. It is the 100-meter hurdles. That first hurdle is now less than ten meters away, and you are approaching it fast.

Anyone who has ever been to a track meet or watched the Olympics understands what happens to a hurdler that fails to get over that first hurdle - - they'll never cross over the following nine, which would allow them to approach the finish line a little more than ten meters past that tenth hurdle.

Some would laugh at this simplified analogy, for though the race is indeed one with obstacles, it might be more likened to a marathon with many, many hurdles along the course.

The good news is this:

You are in the race.

You are on your way.

And you are not running alone.

The adventure before you is a ride *and* a race. Enjoy both aspects of the journey.

In the next chapter we will meet someone who will also, like your realtor, cheer you on and be a coach that will guide you toward the results you are looking for. They will be there each step of the way to lend a helping hand.

Fittingly, they are referred to as: the lender.

Chapter Two: Adding Another Coach

As you will discover, buying a home involves a team of people working together. There is no one more crucial in lending a hand to you and your realtor than a mortgage lender. This is the person who works with the financial institution, or mortgage bank, that offers your home loan.

Your first coach is your realtor. Your second coach is your lender. They work together to make this race a victorious one.

Some may make preparations before the homeowner's race begins by working with their bank regarding a pre-approval, or some form of pre-qualification, which helps them understand how much you can afford to spend.

You may wonder where to start. Don't feel bad about that. This is a learning process. Together we will run this race one step at a time.

Your real estate agent has built relationships with local lenders and can point you in the right direction, making the necessary connections to help you start working with a trusted lender. Believe me when I say your realtor has more than likely worked with good ones and bad ones. They know who to work with for your benefit. This is so important.

A good lender will be very accessible to you. If they do not return your calls or texts in a timely fashion they are not the lender for you. If days go by and you have not heard back from them, consider this a large red flag. Your lender needs to respond to you.

You need a lender who will be patient with you, talk to you throughout the process, which they know and understand. This only comes with experience. You, as the consumer, may not be familiar with the lingo, the words, the terminology, the ins and outs of all it will take to accomplish what needs to be done.

Be prepared for blunt honesty. This is for your benefit. A good lender wants you to understand the reality of what you are walking into. It cannot be stressed strongly enough how important a good lender is for you.

Knowledge is key. Your realtor needs to align you with someone they trust, and that you can trust. Remember, this is one of your coaches, and you need someone who will be there with you every step of the way.

Once you have established who your lender is you are ready to proceed through the **Four C's**. In the following pages, we will walk through each of them in more detail. They are:

CREDIT:
Your financial status and
how you pay your debts

CAPACITY:
Your ability to buy a home
based on your income

CAPITAL:
Do you have funds
for a down payment?

COLLATERAL:
What the house is worth
and the value of the home

Chapter Three: The First C is Credit

Credit defines your financial status and how you pay your debts.

The best way to start is establishing your pre-approval. ***This is key!*** This will let your realtor and lender know where you stand. This will set a tone for what kind of loan you can get qualified and approved for.

There are some clients who want to look at a house they think they are in love with before getting pre-approved. They love the house, and it is the house for them! After they have decided they have to have the house, they are pre-approved for much less than they need for that house, and their dreams are dashed.

They worked hard building false hope. They wasted their time, their realtor's time, and in the end they find themselves devastated.

Don't be one of these people. There is only one way to avoid this type of scenario:

Pre-approval comes first!

No realtor wants to expend their time, energy, and expense driving you around showing you houses until you are pre-approved. This is the way to show your realtor you are serious about purchasing a home.

Keep in mind, your realtor and your lender are most likely working with multiple clients. You must rise to this level of seriousness to garner their valuable time. A good coach will not want to train you until you are determined to run the race.

For some, a pre-approval can happen within an hour or so. For others, it may take several days. It all depends on how quickly you can supply your lender with the documentation they need to move ahead. The more information you can provide up front, the better qualified they are to establish your financial status, which will determine what you can afford for a monthly house payment.

Your lender wants to know **everything** about your financial status! Don't be shy about sharing this information. Be upfront and honest: tell them **everything**. They are not concerned about your personal information, other than to use it to structure your loan in the easiest way possible with the least amount of resistance or stress. Remember, a good lender is looking out for your best interest.

The more information they are given, the good, the bad and the ugly (and everything else in between), will help your lender know how to structure your loan.

The following four steps are necessary to help you move toward **pre-qualification**. After you have been pre-qualified your lender will verify all the information you submitted. Only then will you become **pre-approved**. Note that pre-qualification, and pre-approval, are two different things.

Being pre-qualified indicates you potentially have the ability to be recognized for financing, but does not guarantee you will be. After the lender can verify all your information, you will become a more legitimate prospect, showing you do have the proper credentials: pre-approved.

Are you ready to get started? Here we go.

Step 1: Gathering General Information

Your lender can send you a secured link via e-mail where you can enter your information, or they can do it for you over the phone. Your lender will need the following information:

- Your name
- Your date of birth
- Your social security number
- Your two-year work history
- Your two-year living history
- The current status of your bank account
  - Are you overdrawn in your account?
  - Do you have money for a down payment or not?
- Are you a veteran?
  If so, you might qualify for a VA loan.

Let me add that if you are self-employed, this becomes a little more tricky as your lender must see all schedules of the Federal 1040 tax returns before pursuing pre-approval. The reason for this is that self-employed clients must be considered by their net income, not their gross income. If they claimed to make $100,000 a year, but then write off $90,000, that means they only made $10,000 of income. You can see how this changes the availability of funds.

This information is needed so your lender can proceed.

Step 2: Pulling your Credit Report

Now some people are leery, maybe even paranoid about having their credit pulled. Some have heard that if they get their credit report pulled, it will damage their credit. In my opinion, this is a myth, it is not totally true. The truth is when your credit report is pulled, the most it will bring your credit score down is three points per pull.

There are times in life when this action is necessary. This is definitely one of those times. If you are serious about purchasing a home, this is definitely part of the process. This will show your lender what you owe and your credit history. This is important.

The **Credit Report** will show the following:
- Credit scores
- Total monthly debt which is needed to determine a debt-to-income ratio
- How debt has been paid
- Past bankruptcies
- Any items in collection or default

The first item on the list is your credit score. This shows an overall view regarding how you have paid debt back over the last seven to ten years.

Credit scores range from 300 to 900.

A 600 credit score tells the lender you are 60% likely to pay your debt. If your score is 650, you are 65% likely to pay your debt. For the lending institution, it gives them an idea as to how likely they are to regain their investment.

To sum it up, this is a complete record of the past seven to ten years of your financial history. Without this knowledge the lender cannot move ahead.

Step 3: Gathering Income Documentation

Your lender needs to be assured you have income. The following needs to be sent to your lender:

- Last 30 days of paystubs
- Last 2 years of W-2 forms
- Last 2 months of bank statements, all pages
- Two years of federal tax returns
  if you are self-employed

Step 4: Calculating your Debt-to-Income Ratio

Based on your income and your credit your debt-to-income ratio can be calculated. This is determined by looking at your gross income compared to your outgoing debts which will include the following:

- Car payment
- Student loan payment
- Any bill where you have taken on credit
  that needs to be paid back
- Child support
- Court garnishments on your paycheck

Lenders look at those financial responsibilities where you have taken out loans or received credit that you need to pay back on a monthly basis.

Lenders look at all debt you pay on a monthly basis. This **does not** include such payments as utility bills, car insurance, phone bill, etc.

This will help you understand how much you can afford for a house payment. That is the big question you need to resolve.

If you are wanting to purchase a $300,000 home, but you only want a monthly house payment of $1,000, you are really saying you can afford a $200,000 home. The mathematics don't add up otherwise. So it all comes down to the monthly payment based on the numbers.

Keep this in mind:

Your lender's job is to manage your expectation of what you want to achieve in buying a house, and where you want to be financially.

Establishing your monthly house payment amount also helps your realtor understand financially what type of house they need to be looking for on your behalf. In the long run, this will help you find the house you can afford much quicker.

Again, the realtor and the lender are your coaches. They are working together as a team to help you run this race of purchasing a home. A good realtor and lender are in constant communication. Their game plan must be coordinated so you can be victorious.

Once you are pre-approved, the lender will supply your realtor with all documentation defining your pre-approval terms.

Your pre-approval is good for 90 days.
The credit report is good for 120 days.

Getting the pre-approval will now give you 90 days to shop for a home and get under contract. If you can settle on a home within three months, that will give your lender 30 days to complete the loan process.

If you go beyond these time limitations, you have to go through the whole process again. Surely that is not what you want to do. So have fun shopping and be ready to find your home!

Before we get ahead of ourselves, let's quickly review the next of the Four C's, as it walks hand and hand with Credit.

Chapter Four: The Second C is Capacity

Capacity defines your ability to buy a home based on your income.

Your lender will need to know what your **income** looks like. This gives them some hints as to your ability to pay for your home. Even with good credit, you will not qualify for financing without income.

If someone has $1,000 monthly income and has a $300 a month car payment, how will they afford to pay a $1,000 house payment? This would be a bad investment on the lender's side, and all the time and energy exerted in looking at homes may be pointless.

The lender may also question whether there is someone willing to co-sign for the loan and be able to shoulder the weight of the debt if need be.

You have to understand that this all leads toward setting up financing for you. What kind of loan should you get? And what loans are available? Your credit score, your income, how much money you have in the bank, and the current interest rates, are all determinations that have to be evaluated.

Each loan has its own guidelines and parameters of what it allows. For example, you must be two years past a chapter 7 bankruptcy date before you can be considered for mortgage financing. (Chapter 13 bankruptcy is different.)

Another example would be someone who has a variable income and work hours that change from week to week. In order to qualify for a mortgage you must work in a specific classification of work for a year as your average income will need to be calculated over time.

A lender's job is to know all these guidelines and parameters so they can best guide you toward a loan for which you are qualified, and one that is right for you. It is so important to work with a trusted professional who understands all the caveats involved in the financing realm.

Something important to also understand is that even the guidelines and parameters shared in this book are likely to change based on what might happen in the industry. This is commonly based on the economy, trends in how loans are being paid back, and other variables. These changes are safeguards applied by financial institutions who are seeking to better protect their investments. You may see changes in each type of loan on a yearly basis.

A good lender will be up to date with any changes or alterations to standards, regulations and guidelines. Remember, a good lender is your coach, and they are extremely important at this point of the race.

The following is a basic overview of the type of loan financing that may be available to you. This will give you a starting point to understand these loan options.

Option 1: The Conventional Loan

The **Conventional loan** is one of the most popular types of mortgages and almost all lenders offer them. In August 2020, 82% of all closed mortgages were conventional loans, according to a report by Ellie Mae Inc., a software company that processes 35% of U.S. mortgage applications.

If you have a good credit score, 680 or higher, money for a down payment, and you have not had any foreclosures or bankruptcies in the previous four years, you will more than likely want a Conventional loan.

Of course, there are also some guidelines with this loan. With conventional financing you need to look at your outgoing debt. When you add up your current loan obligations and your proposed house payment, this amount cannot exceed 50% of your gross income (what you make before taxes).

This loan requires a minimum of 3% down payment of the purchase price of the home. This does not include closing costs.

Gift funds may be used for the down payment. This means a family member, employer, or a close family friend may give a monetary gift that can be used. A paper trail must verify how the funds were obtained, and transferred, for this purpose.

This loan is commonly seen as the easiest loan, with the least amount of resistance for the seller. But this doesn't necessarily mean it is the best route for the buyer. This is where a good lender will lead you toward your best option.

This is not a government insured loan.

Option 2: The FHA Loan

An **FHA loan** (Federal Housing Administration) will consider those who have a credit score as low as 580, and requires a down payment of 3.5% of the purchase price. If your credit score is between 500 and 579, a 10% down payment is required.

Here are several guidelines associated with this loan:

- The home must be the borrower's primary residence.
- You must have steady income and proof of employment.
- You are not eligible for FHA financing if you have filed bankruptcy in the previous two years.
- PMI (Premium Mortgage Insurance) is required until 20% of the appraised value is paid.

FHA loans are a good option for first-time homebuyers who do not have a large down payment.

This is a government-insured loan. This does not mean you go to the government to get approved, it means the government is insuring the loan. The bank is lending you the money, but if you default on your mortgage, the government is giving an insurance policy to the lender so they will get repaid. This also applies for a VA loan and a USDA loan, which we will cover next.

Option 3: The USDA Loan

A **USDA loan** (United States Department of Agriculture) promotes homeownership in rural areas, places consisting of a density of less than 500 people per square mile. This loan is population restrictive and is geared toward those who are in the low-to-moderate income bracket looking for a primary residence.

As previously stated, like the FHA loan, this is also a government-insured loan.

Due to yearly changing census reports, the areas that qualify may change on a regular basis. If you want to check the availability in your area for a USDA loan, you can log in to their website, type in the home address, and it will let you see if the property may qualify. The USDA link is:

https://eligibility.sc.egov.usda.gov/eligibility/welcomeAction.do

Since this is a 100% financed loan and does not require a down payment, a credit score of 640 or above is needed.

There are income restrictions with the USDA loan, and they may differ from county to county. After establishing how many people are in your household, you may be limited to $100,000.00 for your total household income.

Your lender will know the details for current guidelines and income restrictions in your area.

Option 4: The VA Loan

A **VA loan** (Department of Veteran Affairs) is a great option for you if you or your spouse meet the minimum service requirements set by the Department of Veterans Affairs (VA), have a valid Certificate of Eligibility (COE), and satisfy the lender's credit and income requirements.

Even if you are in the reserves and are called to active duty in another country even for one day, you would qualify for a VA loan.

This loan offers 100% financing without charging PMI (Premium Mortgage Insurance), which is used to protect the lender if you stop making payments on your loan.

Again, as previously stated, like the FHA loan, this is also a government insured loan.

You will rely heavily on your lender to determine which loan is best for you. Keep in mind, every loan is like a puzzle. Are you a 300 piece puzzle or a 1,000 piece puzzle? And how you put it together matters.

Chapter Five: The Third C is Capital

Capital determines whether or not you have funds for a down payment.

Your bank statements will show how much money you have access to. The funds you have will strengthen your position as a buyer, as you will have something for a down payment, if needed, and something to fall back on if you fall on hard times.

This is what we mean by capital: your assets.

Your financial status is determined by:

- The balance in your bank accounts
- Inheritance
- 401K funds
- Tax return money
- Monetary gifts from family

Now that you have cleared all the hurdles of getting pre-approved, you and your realtor will have a good idea where you stand and what you can afford monthly for a house payment.

As your lender takes a step back, it's time for you to step it up and have some fun. It's time to go shopping - *for your home!*

Chapter Six: Shop 'Til You Drop

Can you guess what is the most expensive purchase ever made? It has been claimed that after twelve years to conceptualize and design, the International Space Station was constructed at a value of $150,000,000,000. For a crew of seven people, it is a very expensive residence with a price tag that is out of this world.

The cost of a home is a little different back here on Earth. The house you buy will surely be less than $267,857,714 per square foot. It will, however, be one of life's biggest purchases.

Did you know that 44% of your lifetime capital is spent on housing? For you, it's **the Real Deal**. So as you start to shop for your home, make sure you enjoy the process. Look, look, look. This is where your realtor will shine, literally walking you through options to consider based on what you can afford.

Keep in mind:

You have 90 days until your pre-approval expires.

Push forward and work with your realtor. This is not a pair of pants you can just take back if you decide it's not a good fit. No one knows for sure how long of a commitment this might be, but plan on finding a place you intend to live in for a while.

In Chapter 1 we talked about some of the non-negotiable essentials that are important to you and your home. As you look at those items, be aware of other areas you may not have thought of. They may not be readily visible until you look for them. These items will typically be part of your home inspection, which we will discuss later. They are important, so look with investigative eyes.

The following is not a comprehensive list, but some of the more important things to consider when shopping for a home, are listed here alphabetically:

- Branches overhanging the roof
- Downspouts
- Driveways, sidewalks and patios
- Electrical
- Exterior Paint
- Fencing
- Foundation issues
- Gutters
- Heat Ventilation and Air Conditioning
- Improper ground grading
- Moisture issues
- Plumbing
- Roof
- Water heater
- Windows

The shopping part of purchasing a home is one of the most exciting pieces in this puzzle. Although this is a race, you may want to slow down here and pace yourself. You may even want to walk or slow to a stop. Enjoy this time of exploration. You may be close to finding a house that will be your home.

Never forget:

There's no place like home.

Chapter Seven: Let the Bartering Begin!

In some foreign countries you may find yourself shopping in a street market where prices on any given item are not set in stone.

The for sale price may be ten dollars.

You could offer five.

A counter offer may let you have it for seven.

Then you could walk away paying six.

This is the art of bartering. I have tried this at Walmart, and it doesn't work. But such a scenario is applicable in buying a home.

After your realtor helps you find a house you want to purchase, it's time to make an offer. **Let the bartering begin!**

The obvious question before you is this: Where should you start in making an offer? It all depends on the house.

How long has the house been on the market? If it is a new listing, a much lower offer may not be considered. I have seen early low offers presented where the seller did not even have the courtesy to respond. At the early stage, right when a house hits the market, it is too soon for overly low bids.

Potential buyers are always waiting to see what comes up for sale, looking at houses as soon as they appear on the market. If a house has been on the market for two or three weeks, a lower offer is something the seller would be more likely to consider.

If a home has been on the market for several months, even unusual offers might be more appropriate. You never know what the seller might consider under those circumstances.

I will never forget a client who was dead set on a certain house. It had been on the market about fifty days or so. It was actually a farm that had been in the listing agent's family for generations. This was a very personal and emotional matter for them. Surely selling such a property would be difficult, parting with a place that held so much nostalgia.

My client insisted on making an offer that I was very uncomfortable writing. It was ridiculously low. I did not believe, with the family circumstances, that such an offer would be welcomed or considered. When I sent it to the listing agent, I immediately texted her with the following message: "I just sent you an offer. Please do not shoot the messenger."

The listing agent called me the following morning. She told me she had a dream that night that told her to accept the next offer made on the farm.

I was so surprised when they agreed to the price. My client made the deal of the century.

Making a low bid can sometimes pay off.

Anything is possible.

You just never know.

You may find a house that you feel is definitely the one for you. Depending on the market, which your realtor will understand, you might want to secure a good offer by staying closer to the asking price.

If homes in the market are selling quickly, you might want to talk with your realtor about establishing an escalation clause when making an offer. This clause states how high you are willing to go regarding the purchase price of the home if a bidding war ensues. Everyone involved in the sale of the home will be aware of this, with the understanding it is not applicable unless they are approached with a higher legitimate offer, proven by a written purchase agreement.

The whole process of making the offer and following it through until you can come to terms is where a good realtor will really shine.

Part of your purchase agreement will include a good faith payment to show you are serious about the offer. This is called "earnest money." The amount is determined by the buyer, based on what they have in their bank account, and is typically between $500 and $10,000, relative to the home price. This is money you need to have available as the listing agent's broker will put your check in trust until closing. The earnest money will be deducted from the home sale price.

If something changes due to your home inspection (which we will talk about in the next chapter), you could get this money back. If, during this process, you were to lose your job and no longer qualify for your loan, you could also get the money back.

If, however, you change your mind about purchasing the home, you will most likely forfeit that money. The earnest money basically takes the home off the market for the seller, so if you walk away, you have delayed the sale of their home. As a result, they could be entitled to keep the earnest money.

Once you receive an accepted offer the interest rate is locked in. Then based on the purchase price, property taxes, and homeowner's insurance (the principle and the interest), your lender can calculate your monthly house payment.

The next step is to have someone look over the house with a fine-tooth comb. Let me introduce you to a professional home inspector.

37

Chapter Eight: Check out the House

A home inspection is an examination of the condition of the house. A home inspector will be looking for issues that may be either costly or dangerous.

Again, your realtor can direct you to inspectors they have worked with and have built trust with.

This may cost between $300 to $1,000, but is worth the investment. Nearly 90% of home inspections will uncover something that needs to be addressed. Most commonly this will involve the roof, windows, and electrical issues.

Once the home inspection has been done the inspector will provide a home inspection report. Prepare for it to be very thorough. A partial list of inspection items was written in Chapter 6 on Page 33. Other areas may be inspected upon request, like:

- Mold
- Radon
- Termite damage
- Water samples
- Well
- Septic

The inspection report will give you recommendations based on the findings.

Discovering these issues may dissuade you from buying the house, or they may be helpful insights as to what you may ask the seller to address before you continue with the purchase.

The seller may agree to make all repairs or some of the repairs. Here's where bartering skills will come in handy and your realtor will shine, negotiating on your behalf.

Be prepared for another possible scenario. The seller may decide to pass on doing any repairs and simply offer funds you can use to do the repairs yourself after you close on the home.

Without the home inspection these issues would more than likely come to light after you buy the house, and then you are on your own. You can see how this smart investment could save you thousands of dollars.

As you read through this book you might have wondered if we forgot the fourth C. Wasn't there supposed to be four? We already looked at **Credit**, **Capacity**, and **Capital**. It is now time to tackle the fourth C, which looks at the value of your home: **Collateral**.

Chapter Nine: The Fourth C is Collateral

Collateral defines what is the value of your home. This is the same as your home appraisal.

The market value of your home needs to be determined to define the collateral against your loan.

Here's what that means:

When you purchase a home, the County Recorder's Office has recorded your mortgage, which is public record. So, there is a lien against the property: your mortgage. If you do not pay your house payments, your house will be seized and sold to pay off the debt.

Or in other words, using an industry wide term:

You don't pay, you don't stay.

So the value of the property needs to be established to determine the financial limits of the loan amount. This is done through an appraisal report, which will include an image of the exterior of the home and a map showing the home's location.

Your lender will order the report, which is created by an unbiased third party professional licensed appraiser, and generally paid for by the buyer.

Depending on the size, complexity, value of the house and property, an appraisal report can typically take from one to three weeks to complete. Expect the fee to be in the range of $450 to $600, which will be ordered by your lender.

The appraiser considers the following factors:
- An in-person inspection of the home
- Recent sales of similar properties in your area
- Current market trends
- Specific details of the home, including:
    - Size
    - Condition
    - Floor plans
    - Special features like a
      swimming pool or fireplace, etc.

At this point, you will be given a loan disclosure which includes the following information:
- The loan terms
- Your projected monthly payment
- How much you will pay in fees
- Closing costs

Chapter Ten: Can I Have Your Approval?

Once the loan disclosers are signed and the lender has all the income and banking documents, the loan will go into underwriting. You want to get the underwriter's approval for your loan.

The job of the underwriter is to assess the following issues:
- Your income
- Your assets
- Your monthly payment obligations
- Your payment history

Your lender will submit all the information to the underwriter, a third party, who is associated with the bank. They will review all documents by plugging them into the computer and reiterating all the terms of the loan. Their responsibility is to make sure that the loan they are giving you will get repaid.

During this process your lender is a liaison between you and the bank. If they have done their job correctly, as a loan officer, the package should be nearly perfect, so after the underwriter's review there will be minimal conditions. It is very rare that an underwriter goes through a document and it is released with no conditions.

After the underwriter goes through the document, it becomes conditionally approved. Your loan is approved as long as the listed conditions are met.

Some of the conditions you might anticipate would be:
- Confirmation of income
- Waiting on the appraisal
- If the house is part of inheritance, confirmation is needed through

a death certificate and inheritance
documentation
* Waiting on title work

If the buyer seems to be making money that does not coincide with their paystubs, the underwriter will want to know where that extra income is coming from.

The title company will also do a search on the home looking for judgements or mortgage liens against the property. They want to be sure the seller is legally authorized to sell the property.

You will receive a Closing Disclosure which will provide final details, which include:

* Loan terms
* Your projected monthly payment
* Your closing costs and fees

At this point, several signatures will be needed. Signatures can be done electronically, which is the easiest route. If you have any questions, your lender will help coach you through this process, either over the phone, through a zoom call, or in person.

After the loan is approved and all the conditions of the underwriter have been met, the final hurdle is finally in sight. You are ready to sprint to the finish line as you head toward closing!

Chapter Eleven: The Finish Line

You are now approaching the finish line.

Your closing is the last step before you are given your house keys.

You, along with your realtor and your lender, will meet at the title company with a title representative who is an impartial third party who notarizes all your documents.

They will have to check your ID to make sure you are who you say you are. Be sure to have your driver's license or a valid passport with you.

As you are approaching this final step, it is very important to heed the following information regarding what **NOT** to do right before your closing:

The **DO NOT DO**s:
- **DO NOT** quit your job in the middle of the loan process!
- **DO NOT** switch jobs in the middle of the loan process!
- **DO NOT** give your notice in the middle of the loan process!
- **DO NOT** make any large purchases where they will need to pull a credit report in the middle of the loan process!
- **DO NOT** purchase a new car in the middle of the loan process!
- **DO NOT** take on any new debt in the middle of the loan process!
- **DO NOT** do **ANYTHING** that deals with your financial status until you talk with your

lender first. They will tell you: **"DO NOT DO ANYTHING in the middle of the loan process!!!"**

You can probably sense a theme here, and your realtor and your lender cannot stress this enough:

<u>DO NOT</u> do anything in the middle of the loan process!

If you do, you just might jeopardize everything, and you may have to start the entire process of verifying income, down payment availability, and on and on. **This is so important! DO NOT** do anything in the middle of the loan process that changes your financial status. This could cost you the house.

You are almost there. The last item of business we need to discuss are closing costs, which will vary depending on your loan program.

Keep in mind, your closing costs and your down payment are two totally different things.

The terms for closing costs are negotiated when your realtor makes your offer. Generally speaking, closing costs could include:

- The appraisal
- The buyer's title fees
- Underwriting fees
- Setting up an escrow account for the buyer for property taxes and home owner's insurance
- Inspection costs

You can ask the seller to pay for closing costs, and this can be negotiated in the purchase contract, which is common.

There is also a closing fee from the title company for their work in notarizing all documentation which is generally split evenly between the buyer and the seller, depending on the purchase agreement.

Well, here you are. At this point, you have crossed over the last hurdle and the finish line is right in front of you. Congratulations. You made it!

Everyone is happy at closing.

You are getting keys to the house.

The seller is getting their money.

Everyone walks away happy.

The race is over and you have emerged victorious!

I hope you enjoyed the ride.

Now it is time to move into your new home.

Chapter Twelve: Move It! Move It! Move It!

Now that you have completed the race and have the keys to your new home, it is time to get moving, literally.

Perhaps you have already started the moving process. If you have not, I would recommend packing items in smaller boxes. No one wants to pick up a large box full of books. It is not only awkward to pick up, but difficult to carry up stairs, and definitely hard on the back. And no one wants to be carrying a large, heavy box of dishes when the bottom falls out.

You can purchase small boxes at a store, like Lowe's, at a decent price. And the smaller boxes stack easily in a car, truck, or moving van.

If you also find you are doing a lot of the moving by yourself, without a team to help, these smaller boxes will be appreciated.

You will find that smaller boxes will be easy to break down and store for other uses when you are finished with them.

After you have moved in and had time to settle, I would encourage you to have friends over to celebrate this momentous accomplishment. It is always nice to have friends and family in your home.

Congratulations on finishing the race!

Now it's time to start making lifelong memories.
Cherish them, and enjoy!

Checklist of Things To Do

This checklist will be handy in helping you keep track of all the steps in the process of purchasing your home. They are listed in order so you can check them off as you accomplish each one.

- ☐ List the features you are looking for in a home
- ☐ Pre-Approval
  - ☐ Gathering General Information
    - ☐ Name
    - ☐ Date of Birth
    - ☐ Social Security Number
    - ☐ 2-year Work History
    - ☐ 2-year Living History
    - ☐ Current Status of your Bank Account
    - ☐ The lender pulls your Credit Report
    - ☐ Gather Income Documentation
    - ☐ Last 30 Days of Paystubs
    - ☐ Last 2 years of W2 forms
    - ☐ Last 2 Months Bank Statements
    - ☐ Two years of Federal Tax Returns (for self-employed)

- [ ] List Outgoing Debts *
  - [ ] Car Payment
  - [ ] Student Loan
  - [ ] Bills you have with Credit that need to be repaid
  - [ ] Child Support
  - [ ] Court Garnishments on your Paycheck
- [ ] Shop for a Home with your Realtor
- [ ] Make An Offer and Barter through your Realtor
- [ ] Earnest Money
- [ ] Home Inspection
- [ ] Appraisal
- [ ] Underwriting
- [ ] Homeowner's Insurance
- [ ] Closing Costs
- [ ] Moving
- [ ] Water Account Established
- [ ] Utility Account Established
- [ ] Wastewater Account Established
- [ ] WIFI Account Established
- [ ] Change of Address at the Post Office

* **NOTE:** When your lender pulls your credit they will see what you are paying monthly, although child support and court garnishment of wages are not seen on the credit report.

About the Author

Heather Deal is a lifelong hoosier. She was born in Kokomo and raised in rural Warsaw until moving to the small cottage town of Winona Lake, Indiana, in 2008.

With her team at H Team Dream Homes, she specializes in helping first time home buyers in northern Indiana.

Heather is a snowmobile enthusiast and enjoys traveling.

Century 21 2018 Double Centurion Team Award

2019 Homesnap Excellence in Client Service Award

2019 Google Excellence in Client Service Award

Century 21 Bradley Realty Inc. Top Relentless Team 2020

Homesnap 2020 Excellence in Client Service Award

Century 21 Centurion Team Award

Century 21 Quality Team Service Award

2021 homes.com Excellence in Client Service Award

2021 Homesnap Excellence in Client Service Award

2023 Michiana Top Producer Award

Heather Deal • H Team Dream Homes
1602 S. Saint Andrews Rd. E., Winona Lake, Indiana USA 46590
www.hteamdreamhomes.com

To purchase paperback copies of

The REAL DEAL:
Real Answers to Real Questions
When Buying Your First Home

or to download the audio book version,
please search for this title and/or the author at:

amazon.com

You can also find a direct purchase link at:

www.hteamdreamhomes.com

This book was written in partnership with
Blue Spaghetti LLC, a creative arts company
Warsaw, Indiana. All rights reserved.

2 0 2 4